ESTABLISHED IN THE FAITH

A Discipleship Guide for Discerning and Affirming a Young Person's Faith

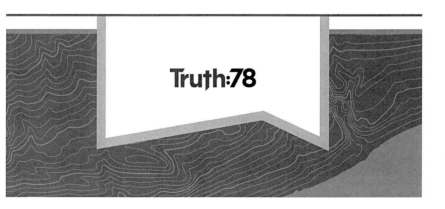

Truth:78

Established in the Faith
A Discipleship Guide for Discerning and Affirming a Young Person's Faith
by David Michael

Copyright © 2001, 2011, 2017, 2019 Next Generation Resources, Inc.
Illustrations Truth78. All rights reserved. No part of this publication may be reproduced in any form without written permission from Truth78.

Published in the United States by Truth78.

All Scripture quotations, unless otherwise noted, are from The Holy Bible, English Standard Version® (ESV®), copyright © 2001 by Crossway, a publishing ministry of Good News Publishers. Used by permission. All rights reserved.

ISBN: 978-0-9969870-8-0

Rev. 5.19

Truth78.org · info@Truth78.org · 877.400.1414 · @Truth78org

Contents

Introduction 4

Step 1: Preparing the Student 11

Step 2: Understanding the Gospel 17

Step 3: Assurance of Salvation 27

Step 4: Affirmation of Faith 33

Step 5: The Meaning of Baptism 37

Step 6: Preparing a Testimony 42

The Ordinance of Baptism 46

When Should a Young Person Be Baptized? 46

Appendix I—Two Views on Childhood Participation in Church Ordinances 47

Appendix II—Concerning the Age of Baptism for Children: Reasons for Waiting 56

Appendix III—What Can Give a Believer Genuine Assurance? 58

Recommended Resources 65

About Truth78 67

Introduction

This guide has roots in three realms of my experience. The first realm was as a boy growing up in a Christian home with godly parents who showed me the way that leads to life (Matthew 7:14). At age seven, I raised my hand to "accept Christ" in a Sunday school class that my mother taught. I have a vague memory of that moment, but no idea what I was thinking or feeling. When we got home that afternoon, she recorded the date in the back of my Bible, marking me as the last of her four children to be saved. It also marked the first of several times while growing up that I "made a decision" or "rededicated my life to the Lord"—never quite sure if I was truly born again. I knew that I was a sinner. I believed that Jesus died for my sins. And I knew that by accepting Jesus "into my heart" I would have eternal life. Looking back, I had a shallow understanding of the gospel and limited confidence in my "decision" to follow Christ. Consequently, I struggled with assurance of salvation for the first two decades of my life.

The second realm was my experience as a father of two daughters. In 1993, my oldest was in sixth grade, and she expressed a desire to be baptized. I was delighted by her interest, but not sure if she was ready. I invited her to a special "daddy-daughter" time to discuss it. We met once a week for seven weeks and reviewed the basics of the Christian faith, baptism, and church membership. She took these sessions seriously, and we were both surprised by how much we enjoyed them. By the time we finished, I was more confident that my daughter was ready for baptism. We also discovered that the time spent in these heartfelt discussions about eternal realities drew us closer as father and daughter, reinforcing a special spiritual bond between us that we both will cherish and benefit from for a lifetime.

Three years later, I was the Pastor for Parenting and Children's Discipleship in my church. In that role, I had the opportunity to influence the way we prepared young people for baptism. I prepared the first edition of this booklet for use by the church and parents as a baptism preparation tool. More importantly, I designed it as a tool that might be used to better discern a young person's understanding of the gospel and where he might be in his spiritual development. Part of my aim in providing this tool is to assist the church in its efforts to faithfully oversee the ordinance of baptism, while preserving and reinforcing the responsibility, privilege, and blessing that belongs to parents to prepare their children to take this important step of obedience and faith.

I have further revised the original material in the hope that it will continue to be useful for baptism preparation, but I also hope it can benefit young people who have already been baptized. I grew up in a church that saw no need for a guide to prepare young people for baptism because, in their view, I had already been baptized when I was three months old. Still, if given the opportunity, I am sure my dad would have welcomed a guide like this and the encouragement to meet with his children to explore their understanding of the truth of the gospel and the state of their souls. I, in turn, would have welcomed the opportunity to discuss these things with my dad. I would have been blessed by those discussions, and I probably would have been spared a lot of confusion and spiritual insecurity.

Nomenclature

One challenge I faced working on this revision was deciding how we should refer to the young person who I hope will benefit from this guide. In the previous editions I used "candidate" (for baptism); but that no longer works since, as already explained, in addition to being a tool for baptism preparation, it has other useful applications. "Child" does not work for those who are older. "Youth" could work, but using it in most sentences is awkward. I came close to using "disciple" because that is how we should think of them, given our desire and responsibility for their faith, as well as our Lord's commission in Matthew 28:19 to "make disciples of all nations." Short of inventing a new word, I settled on "student," which works even though it can imply that this effort is a mere academic exercise. In a further effort to avoid cumbersome wording, I am also following the biblical pattern of using the masculine pronoun inclusively to refer to male and female.

Before You Begin

Like most things in life, you and your student will gain more from this experience if you take time to prepare. Here are five suggestions:

1. *Connect with a pastor/elder in your church.*

If you are using this guide to prepare someone for baptism, it is important to seek the support and involvement of your church leadership. If you have been given this guide as part of your church's baptism preparation process, the connection with your church's leadership is already in place. You may be using this guide as a supplement to your church's discipleship process. In either of these scenarios, connecting with church leadership is fitting, since baptism is most appropriately performed in the context of the local church (1 Corinthians 12:12-13).

2. *Examine yourself and pray.*

You may not consider yourself a shining example of faith, and thus you may feel reluctant to instruct and encourage someone else in his faith. This job does not require you to be a theological or spiritual "giant," but it does require you to lean on the Lord's grace, which "is sufficient for you" (2 Corinthians 12:9). Paul was one of the greatest spiritual mentors of all time, yet he affirmed that his message and preaching "were not in plausible words of wisdom, but in demonstration of the Spirit and of power" (1 Corinthians 2:4), so that his faith was not resting "in the wisdom of men but in the power of God" (1 Corinthians 2:5).

Weakness, however, should not be confused with hypocrisy. It would be difficult to authentically lead a young person through these steps if you are not a believer. So, first follow Paul's admonition and "examine [yourself], to see whether you are in the faith" (2 Corinthians 13:5). Furthermore, we should not presume to give spiritual direction to another person if we are walking in disobedience and deliberately sinning against the Lord. Paul rebukes Roman teachers who taught others but did not teach themselves.

> "If you are trusting Christ, walking in His ways, waging war against sin, and striving to be an example... then pursue this opportunity to encourage another person in his faith..."
> —DAVID MICHAEL

> *Romans 2:21-24—you then who teach others, do you not teach yourself? While you preach against stealing, do you steal? ²²You who say that one must not commit adultery, do you commit adultery? You who abhor idols, do you rob temples? ²³You who boast in the law dishonor God by breaking the law. ²⁴For, as it is written, "The name of God is blasphemed among the Gentiles because of you."*

If you are trusting Christ, walking in His ways, waging war against sin, and striving to be an example to others "in speech, in conduct, in love, in faith, [and] in purity" (1 Timothy 4:12), then pursue this opportunity to encourage another person in his faith and join with the Apostle Paul, who said:

> *2 Corinthians 4:1-2—Therefore, having this ministry by the mercy of God, we do not lose heart. ²But we have renounced disgraceful, underhanded ways. We refuse to practice cunning or to tamper with God's word, but by the open statement of the truth we would commend ourselves to everyone's conscience in the sight of God.*

3. *Enlist prayer support.*

We can lead a person through the steps in this guide, but only God can touch someone's heart and generate an authentic response to truth. Recognize that God may be pleased to use this time to advance His work in your student's life and touch his heart (and yours) in a meaningful and life-changing way. Also, be careful not to underestimate what the enemy of our faith and our souls may do to oppose this work. Invite others to join you in praying that the Lord influence the heart and thwart the efforts of our "ancient foe."[1]

4. *Encourage spiritual discipline.*

If the student does not have a regular time of personal Bible study and prayer, this would be a good time to begin. Along with daily Bible reading and prayer, you may want to assign memory work or homework. You may also want to encourage keeping a journal of thoughts, insights, and highlights gleaned from personal time in the Word and from these sessions together. Consider keeping your own journal as well, to document your thoughts and impressions, including topics discussed, questions raised, observations made, and insights gained throughout this process. Consider spending part of your time together sharing the gleanings from your time in the Word and prayer.

5. *Plan your meeting times.*

It is important for you to set aside sufficient time to meet privately with your student. This will communicate that these times are important and should be taken seriously. Plan at least six sessions. Even though it may be possible to race through the material, I suggest that you spread the sessions over several weeks.

Establish a regular time, and perhaps find a special place to meet. After meeting weekly in a local restaurant to work through this material with his daughter, one dad wrote: "Although I initially approached these sessions with some fear and trepidation, we have had such deep conversations that I am actually looking forward to continuing these, even after baptism! Thanks for helping get us off the dime." If you are a

---

[1] This references a line in Martin Luther's hymn *A Mighty Fortress is Our God.*

parent who is stuck on "the dime," consider that this process may help establish a regular time when your son or daughter can anticipate the opportunity to discuss important issues of life and faith with you.

Preparing for Each Session

There are six steps in this process and, in most cases, each step requires at least one session to complete. Think of the steps as milestones and take as many sessions as you need to reach each one. This guide will provide enough detail to direct you for each session, but it is also flexible enough for you to lead the discussion in a way that works best for you and your student.

1. Preparation

Carefully review the goals for each session ahead of time, and think about how you will guide your student through each session. Keep in mind that this guide is a tool to help you prepare. It is not designed to simply be read to or by the student. Plan for these meetings to be face-to-face and heart-to-heart discussions. Rather than reading aloud from this booklet, it would be better to make your own notes. This will communicate that what you are saying comes from your heart and that you consider these matters serious enough to take the time to prepare.

2. Prayer

Make prayer a significant part of each session. Encourage the student to pray with you. If you are a parent and prayer with your son or daughter has become awkward or mechanical, you may need to give some structure to your prayers. Praying through a particular Bible text is one way to provide form and substance to prayer. There are also simple acrostics that can be helpful such as ACTS[2] or APTAT.[3]

---

[2] Sproul, R.C. "A Simple Acrostic for Prayer: A.C.T.S." June 25, 2018, https://www.ligonier.org/blog/simple-acrostic-prayer/ (accessed 1/11/19)

[3] Piper, John. "Practical Help for Praying for Help," January 3, 1988, https://www.desiringgod.org/messages/practical-help-for-praying-for-help (accessed 1/11/19)

3. Application

For each session, your aim should be to influence not only the "head" but also the "heart." It is important for the student to understand the truth, but his heart response to the truth is even more important. Look and listen for an authentic heart response to the things you discuss together.

Step 1: Preparing the Student

1.1 Goal

The goal in this step is to prepare the student for the time you will spend together. The aim is to clarify expectations and to impress upon him the significance of the discussion you will be having. The hope is that, by the time this first meeting comes to an end, the student will realize these meetings are important and resolve to take them seriously.

1.2 Expectations

Begin by making sure the student understands the reason for meeting. Encourage him to describe his expectations for these sessions and what he hopes will come from them. It will also be important for you to talk about your expectations and vision for your time together. For example, you could say something like this:

> *This is a time for us to talk about important issues of faith and obedience. I want to make sure you understand the saving work that I believe the Lord has done in your life, and I want to help you put it into words.*

If the student is being prepared for baptism, you may want to say something like:

> *I want to help you understand what baptism means and make sure you are ready to move ahead with it. You may come to the end of this time and feel ready to be baptized, or you may want to wait. I want you to feel ready, but not pressured into it.*

1.3 A Call to Spiritual Manhood/Womanhood

Consider with the student the following texts from
1 Corinthians and emphasize that the time has come in his life
to start moving away from spiritual childhood.

> *1 Corinthians 3:1-2a—But I, brothers, could not address
> you as spiritual people, but as people of the flesh, as
> infants in Christ. ²I fed you with milk, not solid food, for
> you were not ready for it.*
>
> *1 Corinthians 13:11—When I was a child, I spoke like a
> child, I thought like a child, I reasoned like a child. When
> I became a man, I gave up childish ways.*
>
> *1 Corinthians 14:20—Brothers, do not be children in
> your thinking. Be infants in evil, but in your thinking be
> mature.*
>
> *1 Corinthians 16:13—Be watchful, stand firm in the faith,
> act like men, be strong.*

The student should understand that even though God is the one
who calls us out of spiritual darkness and gives us a heart that
can respond to Him, we must personally respond to God in faith
and walk in obedience. Emphasize that the student must now
take responsibility for himself in ways that he could not when
he was a little child. This analogy may be helpful:

*When you were a baby, you were totally helpless. You
could not be responsible for feeding yourself, cleaning up
after yourself, or keeping yourself warm, because you were
physically unable to do those things. Spiritually you were
also helpless. You were not mature enough, and your brain
was not developed enough to understand sin, your need for
salvation, and all that Jesus did to deliver you from sin. Little
by little, you have been growing in your understanding of
these things so that now you are responsible for acting on the
truth you understand.*

1.4 A Call to Joy

In this first session, and in the ones that follow, it will be helpful to impress upon the student that you are committed to his joy. You want him to be blessed. And you want him to know that blessing flows from both the fear of and the delight in the LORD. We want him to tremble and dance in the presence of the LORD. "Blessed is the man who *fears the LORD*, who *greatly delights* in his commandments!" (Psalm 112:1b).

There are numerous biblical texts you can read together to emphasize that the call to follow the Lord is a call to pursue joy in this life and in the life to come. Psalm 16 is the testimony of a man who feared and delighted in the LORD. Consider this text, or perhaps one of your favorites, emphasizing the joy that the psalmist found in following the LORD.

> *Psalm 16:1-11—Preserve me, O God, for in you I take refuge. ²I say to the LORD, "You are my Lord; I have no good apart from you." ³As for the saints in the land, they are the excellent ones, in whom is all my delight. ⁴The sorrows of those who run after another god shall multiply; their drink offerings of blood I will not pour out or take their names on my lips. ⁵The LORD is my chosen portion and my cup; you hold my lot. ⁶The lines have fallen for me in pleasant places; indeed, I have a beautiful inheritance. ⁷I bless the LORD who gives me counsel; in the night also my heart instructs me. ⁸I have set the LORD always before me; because he is at my right hand, I shall not be shaken. ⁹Therefore my heart is glad, and my whole being rejoices; my flesh also dwells secure. ¹⁰For you will not abandon my soul to Sheol, or let your holy one see corruption. ¹¹You make known to me the path of life; in your presence there is fullness of joy; at your right hand are pleasures forevermore.*

1.5 A Call to Readiness

The Bible clearly teaches that there is a coming judgment.

> *Matthew 25:31-34, 41, 46—"When the Son of Man comes in his glory, and all the angels with him, then he will sit on his glorious throne. ³²Before him will be gathered all the nations, and he will separate people one from another as a shepherd separates the sheep from the goats. ³³And he will place the sheep on his right, but the goats on the left. ³⁴Then the King will say to those on his right, 'Come, you who are blessed by my Father, inherit the kingdom prepared for you from the foundation of the world.'...⁴¹Then he will say to those on his left, 'Depart from me, you cursed, into the eternal fire prepared for the devil and his angels.'...⁴⁶And these will go away into eternal punishment, but the righteous into eternal life."*

> **"You are responsible to point him to the Lord, teach him the truth, and warn him of the coming judgment; but emphasize that you cannot respond for him. You cannot embrace the truth for him. This is something he must do, and he can only do it with God's help and by His grace."**
>
> —DAVID MICHAEL

Make clear to the student that you, as his parent/mentor, have a responsibility for him and for his faith. You are responsible to point him to the Lord, teach him the truth, and warn him of the coming judgment; but emphasize that you cannot respond for him. You cannot embrace the truth for him. This is something he must do, and he can only do it with God's help and by His grace. The following text may help him understand this principle:

> *Ezekiel 33:7-9—"So you, son of man, I have made a watchman for the house of Israel. Whenever you hear a word from my mouth, you shall give them warning from me. ⁸If I say to the wicked, O wicked one, you shall surely die, and you do not speak to warn the wicked to turn from his way, that wicked person shall die in his iniquity, but his blood I will require at your hand. ⁹But if you warn the wicked to turn from his way, and he does not turn from his way, that person shall die in his iniquity, but you will have delivered your soul."*

You then could say something like, "As your [parent/mentor], I am like that watchman. God calls me to faithfully teach and guide you in His way. If I don't do that, you could die in your sin; but the Lord will hold me responsible. If I faithfully lead you to the truth, you could still reject it and die in your sin; but the Lord will not hold me responsible."

We can be certain that Jesus will return, and we can be certain that we will all die unless Jesus returns first. No one knows when either of these things will take place. Consider the following texts:

> *Mark 13:26-27, 32—"And then they will see the Son of Man coming in clouds with great power and glory. ²⁷And then he will send out the angels and gather his elect from the four winds, from the ends of the earth to the ends of heaven...³²But concerning that day or that hour, no one knows, not even the angels in heaven, nor the Son, but only the Father."*

> *Luke 12:19-20—"And I will say to my soul, 'Soul, you have ample goods laid up for many years; relax, eat, drink, be merry.' ²⁰But God said to him, 'Fool! This night your soul is required of you, and the things you have prepared, whose will they be?'"*

> *James 4:13-15—Come now, you who say, "Today or tomorrow we will go into such and such a town and spend a year there and trade and make a profit"—¹⁴yet you do*

> not know what tomorrow will bring. What is your life? For you are a mist that appears for a little time and then vanishes. ¹⁵Instead you ought to say, "If the Lord wills, we will live and do this or that,"

Even though the Bible does not tell us when these things will take place, it does tell us to be prepared. Consider these texts:

> *Mark 13:33-36*—"Be on guard, keep awake. For you do not know when the time will come. ³⁴It is like a man going on a journey, when he leaves home and puts his servants in charge, each with his work, and commands the doorkeeper to stay awake. ³⁵Therefore stay awake—for you do not know when the master of the house will come, in the evening, or at midnight, or when the rooster crows, or in the morning—³⁶lest he come suddenly and find you asleep. ³⁷And what I say to you I say to all: Stay awake."

Also, consider the parable of the 10 virgins waiting for the bridegroom (Matthew 25:1-13) and the parable of the talents (Matthew 25:14-30).

As you conclude this session, share your heart's desire to be ready to meet the Lord when He returns.

Step 2: Understanding the Gospel

2.1 Goal

The goal in this step is to deepen the student's understanding of and appreciation for the gospel, so that by the time he comes to Step 6 in this process, he can articulate a solid understanding of the gospel and express deep affection for it. This is the most important step in the process. Please do not rush through this or settle for a superficial understanding. Many young people growing up among Christians will say that they believe Jesus died for their sins, but they have no idea why sin is a problem and how Jesus' death and resurrection solves the problem for us. They may also affirm that they have "accepted Jesus" or "made a decision for Christ" without really understanding what they must do to personally benefit from the saving work of Christ, and what it means to trust Jesus and follow Him as Lord.

Discerning if your student is embracing the gospel (or merely agreeing with it) can be very difficult. Prayer is always the first step in spiritual discernment. The Appendix of this booklet includes a number of questions that can also be helpful to discern genuine faith. (See "What Can Give a Believer Genuine Assurance" by Wayne Grudem.)

I have provided in this section the key elements of the gospel that the student needs to understand. If you complete this session and sense a need for more time, I recommend working through the Truth78 booklet, *Helping Children to Understand the Gospel*, available from Truth78.org.

2.2 The Gospel Outline

Begin the session by asking the student about his understanding of the gospel. This will help you discern what he already understands and which of the following elements of the gospel you will need to emphasize in your instruction:

- *What is your understanding of who God is and how we should relate to Him?*
- *What is your understanding of sin and the consequences of sin?*
- *Who is Jesus, and why was it important that He never sinned?*
- *Why was Jesus' death necessary?*
- *How does Jesus' death and resurrection accomplish our salvation?*
- *How does God apply the redemption purchased by Christ to us?*
- *What must we do to be saved?*
- *How do we live as a disciple of Christ?*

After discussing each of these elements, encourage the student to put the gospel into his own words. Review often, even outside the session.

One way to frame the gospel for the student is to explain that God's saving work began long before we were born. The decisive point of salvation was at the cross, not when we personally came to Christ. Your job is to help the student understand and be able to describe what Christ did at the cross and resurrection to save him, how God works in a person's life to bring him into this salvation, and the implications of daily trusting and following Christ.

Another way to frame the gospel is to explain that there was a problem that needed to be solved, what God did to solve it, and how we come to benefit from the solution.

Any way you frame your explanation of the gospel, there are four essential elements the student must understand and be able to put into words.

1. Truth about God

God is the sovereign Creator of all things.

Because God created all things, He is the owner and ruler of all things, including every person.

> *Psalm 24:1—The earth is the LORD's and the fullness thereof, the world and those who dwell therein,*

> *1 Chronicles 29:11—Yours, O LORD, is the greatness and the power and the glory and the victory and the majesty, for all that is in the heavens and in the earth is yours. Yours is the kingdom, O LORD, and you are exalted as head above all.*

God is holy.

God is perfect in every way; He does not sin, do evil, or make mistakes. God is righteous—right in all He thinks, says, and does.

> *Deuteronomy 32:4—The Rock, his work is perfect, for all his ways are justice. A God of faithfulness and without iniquity, just and upright is he.*

> *Isaiah 5:16—But the LORD of hosts is exalted in justice, and the Holy God shows himself holy in righteousness.*

God is separated from sin.

Because God is holy and righteous, sin cannot abide in His presence; to be holy is to be completely separated from sin. When Adam and Eve sinned, they hid from the presence of the Lord. The "holy of holies" in the tabernacle and temple reminded Israel that God was separated from them because He is holy.

> *Habakkuk 1:13a—You who are of purer eyes than to see evil and cannot look at wrong,*

Because God is holy, we must be holy, too.

In order to live in right relationship with God, we must be holy and blameless in His sight.

> *1 Peter 1:15-16—but as he who called you is holy, you also be holy in all your conduct, ¹⁶since it is written, "You shall be holy, for I am holy."*

> *Ephesians 1:4—...[God] chose us in him before the foundation of the world, that we should be holy and blameless before him...*

God's laws and commands are holy and righteous because they have been shaped by His character. The commands show us what is pleasing and acceptable conduct to a holy God.

> *Romans 7:12—So the law is holy, and the commandment is holy and righteous and good.*

> *Psalm 119:160—The sum of your word is truth, and every one of your righteous rules endures forever.*

God is devoted to His glory.

Everything God has done, all that He is doing, and all that He ever will do is for His glory—for displaying His greatness and worth.

> *Romans 11:36—For from him and through him and to him are all things. To him be glory forever. Amen.*

> *Isaiah 42:8—I am the LORD; that is my name; my glory I give to no other, nor my praise to carved idols.*

> *1 Chronicles 29:11— Yours, O LORD, is the greatness and the power and the glory and the victory and the majesty, for all that is in the heavens and in the earth is yours. Yours is the kingdom, O LORD, and you are exalted as head above all.*

God created us for His glory.

God created us in His image and likeness for His glory.

> *Genesis 1:26-27—Then God said, "Let us make man in our image, after our likeness. And let them have dominion over the fish of the sea and over the birds of the heavens and over the livestock and over all the earth and over every creeping thing that creeps on the earth." [27]So God created man in his own image, in the image of God he created him; male and female he created them.*

> *Isaiah 43:6b, 7b—"...bring my sons from afar and my daughters from the end of the earth. [7]...whom I created for my glory..."*

Because we were made for God's glory, we must live for His glory.

As God's image bearers, we were created to know, honor and treasure God most of all, reflecting His greatness and worth.

> *Psalm 86:11-12—Teach me your way, O LORD, that I may walk in your truth; unite my heart to fear your name. [12]I give thanks to you, O Lord my God, with my whole heart, and I will glorify your name forever.*

> *1 Corinthians 10:31—So, whether you eat or drink, or whatever you do, do all to the glory of God.*

2. Truth about Sin

Sin is failure to conform perfectly to God's law and to glorify Him.

> *Romans 3:20—For by works of the law no human being will be justified in his sight, since through the law comes knowledge of sin.*

> *James 2:10—For whoever keeps the whole law but fails in one point has become guilty of all of it.*

> *Romans 1:21—For although they knew God, they did not honor him as God or give thanks to him, but they became*

futile in their thinking, and their foolish hearts were darkened.

Because of Adam's sin, we all, as human beings, are born with a corrupt nature, which means we are born sinful.

Romans 5:12—Therefore, just as sin came into the world through one man, and death through sin, and so death spread to all men because all sinned—

Because of our sin, we all fail to please God.

Romans 8:7-8—For the mind that is set on the flesh is hostile to God, for it does not submit to God's law; indeed, it cannot. ⁸Those who are in the flesh cannot please God.

We have failed to be holy.

Romans 3:10-12—…"None is righteous, no, not one; ¹¹no one understands; no one seeks for God. ¹²All have turned aside; together they have become worthless; no one does good, not even one."

We have failed to glorify God.

Romans 3:23—for all have sinned and fall short of the glory of God,

We do not love God as we should, trust Him as we should, treasure Him as we should, or honor Him as we should.

Because of our sin, God is rightly angry with us.

Romans 2:5—But because of your hard and impenitent heart you are storing up wrath for yourself on the day of wrath when God's righteous judgment will be revealed.

Ephesians 2:1, 3b—And you were dead in the trespasses and sins ³…and were by nature children of wrath, like the rest of mankind.

Ephesians 5:6b—…the wrath of God comes upon the sons of disobedience.

Because of our sin, we are under the wrath of God and condemned to eternal punishment in hell.

> *2 Thessalonians 1:9—They* [those who do not know God, and those who do not obey the gospel] *will suffer the punishment of eternal destruction, away from the presence of the Lord and from the glory of his might,*

3. Truth about Christ

Christ is the Son of God. He is fully God and became fully man.

> *John 1:1—In the beginning was the Word, and the Word was with God, and the Word was God.*

> *John 1:14—And the Word became flesh and dwelt among us, and we have seen his glory, glory as of the only Son from the Father, full of grace and truth.*

Christ is holy and righteous. He perfectly obeyed the law. (Jesus is sinless.)

> *Hebrews 4:15—For we do not have a high priest who is unable to sympathize with our weaknesses, but one who in every respect has been tempted as we are, yet without sin.*

> *John 8:29—"And he* [God] *who sent me* [Jesus] *is with me. He has not left me alone, for I always do the things that are pleasing to him."*

Christ took our sins upon Himself. He became a curse for us and received the wrath of God in our place.

Christ became our substitute through His death on the cross. He became the object of God's wrath and took our punishment.

> *1 Peter 2:24—He himself bore our sins in his body on the tree, that we might die to sin and live to righteousness. By his wounds you have been healed.*

> *Isaiah 53:5-6—But he was pierced for our transgressions; he was crushed for our iniquities; upon him was the chastisement that brought us peace, and with his wounds we are healed. ⁶All we like sheep have gone astray; we have turned—every one—to his own way; and the LORD has laid on him the iniquity of us all.*

> *Galatians 3:13a—Christ redeemed us from the curse of the law by becoming a curse for us...*

Christ gives to His people His perfect righteousness.

In Christ, we become holy and blameless in God's sight.

> *2 Corinthians 5:21—For our sake he made him to be sin who knew no sin, so that in him we might become the righteousness of God.*

> *Romans 5:19—For as by the one man's disobedience the many were made sinners, so by the one man's obedience the many will be made righteous.*

Christ's resurrection was proof of His victory over sin and death, opening the way of eternal life.

> *Romans 6:9—We know that Christ, being raised from the dead, will never die again; death no longer has dominion over him.*

4. Truth about Salvation

Salvation is by grace alone; it is a gift of God.

> *Ephesians 2:8b-9—And this is not your own doing; it is the gift of God, ⁹not a result of works, so that no one may boast.*

> *Romans 3:23-24—for all have sinned and fall short of the glory of God, ²⁴and are justified by his grace as a gift, through the redemption that is in Christ Jesus,*

Faith is the way we benefit from what Jesus did for us.

> *Ephesians 2:8a—For by grace you have been saved through faith.*
>
> *John 3:16—For God so loved the world, that he gave his only Son, that whoever believes in him should not perish but have eternal life.*

Faith is trusting in Christ alone for the forgiveness of our sins and the fulfillment of all His promises to us.

> *Titus 3:4-7—But when the goodness and loving kindness of God our Savior appeared, ⁵he saved us, not because of works done by us in righteousness, but according to his own mercy, by the washing of regeneration and renewal of the Holy Spirit, ⁶whom he poured out on us richly through Jesus Christ our Savior, ⁷so that being justified by his grace we might become heirs according to the hope of eternal life.*

Faith is always accompanied by repentance, a deep-felt sorrow, and hatred of sin, such that you turn to Jesus and commit to follow Him.

> *2 Corinthians 7:10—For godly grief produces a repentance that leads to salvation without regret, whereas worldly grief produces death.*
>
> *Mark 1:15b—"...repent and believe in the gospel."*

Faith results in loving and treasuring Christ above all.

> *Philippians 3:8-9—Indeed, I count everything as loss because of the surpassing worth of knowing Christ Jesus my Lord. For his sake I have suffered the loss of all things and count them as rubbish, in order that I may gain Christ ⁹and be found in him, not having a righteousness of my own that comes from the law, but that which comes through faith in Christ, the righteousness from God that depends on faith—*

True faith is evidenced by a growing desire to obey Christ and please Him in all we do.

> *Ephesians 2:8-10—For by grace you have been saved through faith. And this is not your own doing; it is the gift of God, ⁹not a result of works, so that no one may boast. ¹⁰For we are his workmanship, created in Christ Jesus for good works, which God prepared beforehand, that we should walk in them.*
>
> *John 14:15—"If you love me, you will keep my commandments."*

2.3 Treasuring Christ Together

We want the student to understand the gospel and be able to communicate it in a coherent and personal way. However, the ability to know, understand, and articulate the gospel does not necessarily point to authentic faith. A young person can memorize the elements of the gospel and the supporting texts without ever treasuring Christ as his own.

As you review the gospel with the student, take time to glory in the love and work of Christ.

Pause from time to time to pray, worship, and give thanks to the Lord. Perhaps look at some hymns or worship songs that help express affection for Christ and for the gospel.

Let the student see your emotion. Let him hear how you express your love for Christ.

Consider giving your own testimony of how you came to understand and cherish the gospel. Encourage him to ask others to share how the gospel became precious to them.

Step 3: Assurance of Salvation

3.1 Goal

In this step, your goal is to help the student "examine [himself], to see whether [he is] in the faith" (2 Corinthians 13:5a). If he is in the faith, then this step will help to strengthen his assurance.

Young people who have grown up in Christian homes and have had early experiences with the Lord often struggle with assurance of salvation. They may be thinking about or asking questions like, "Did I really know what I was doing at six years old when I accepted Jesus in my heart? Do I believe just because I was taught to believe a certain way, or am I genuinely and personally trusting in Christ?"

In this step, it will be important for the student to have ample opportunity to express any questions or doubts with which he may be wrestling. Encourage him to be open and honest about his thoughts and feelings concerning the Lord. Assure him that any sincere question is a good question.

3.2 Can I lose my salvation?

First, establish that a true Christian—a person who is truly treasuring Christ—will not fall away, but will persevere in faith to the end of his life. Consider together the following texts:

> *John 6:38-40—"For I have come down from heaven, not to do my own will but the will of him who sent me. *39*And this is the will of him who sent me, that I should lose nothing of all that he has given me, but raise it up on the last day. *40*For this is the will of my Father, that everyone who looks on the Son and believes in him should have eternal life, and I will raise him up on the last day."*

> *John 8:31—So Jesus said to the Jews who had believed in him, "If you abide in my word, you are truly my disciples,"*

> *John 10:27-29—"My sheep hear my voice, and I know them, and they follow me. ^{28}I give them eternal life, and they will never perish, and no one will snatch them out of my hand. ^{29}My Father, who has given them to me, is greater than all, and no one is able to snatch them out of the Father's hand."*
>
> *Colossians 1:21-23—And you, who once were alienated and hostile in mind, doing evil deeds, ^{22}he has now reconciled in his body of flesh by his death, in order to present you holy and blameless and above reproach before him, ^{23}if indeed you continue in the faith, stable and steadfast, not shifting from the hope of the gospel that you heard, which has been proclaimed in all creation under heaven, and of which I, Paul, became a minister.*
>
> *Hebrews 3:12-14—Take care, brothers, lest there be in any of you an evil, unbelieving heart, leading you to fall away from the living God. ^{13}But exhort one another every day, as long as it is called "today," that none of you may be hardened by the deceitfulness of sin. ^{14}For we have come to share in Christ, if indeed we hold our original confidence firm to the end.*

3.3 How can I know if my faith is real?

If we can have confidence that a true believer is secure in Christ, ask the student to consider how we can know if a person is truly a believer or not? *How do we know if our faith or someone else's faith is real?*

In Chapter 40 of *Systematic Theology: An Introduction to Biblical Doctrine*, Wayne Grudem offers three practical questions to help us discern genuine faith. I introduce these questions briefly in this section, but the entire article with supporting texts and further explanation is included in Appendix III of this booklet. *If you have time, we highly recommend that you review the full text of Grudem's article and work through some of the related verses with the student.*

Do I have a present trust in Christ for salvation?

"Do I today have trust in Christ to forgive my sins and take me without blame into heaven forever? Do I have confidence in my heart that he has saved me? If I were to die tonight and stand before God's judgment seat, and if he were to ask me why he should let me into heaven, would I begin to think of my good deeds and depend on them, or would I without hesitation say that I am depending on the merits of Christ and am confident that he is a sufficient Savior?"[4]

Is there evidence of a regenerating work of the Holy Spirit in my heart?

Grudem suggests six evidences of this regenerating work:[5]

1. *First, there is a subjective testimony of the Holy Spirit within our hearts bearing witness that we are God's children (Rom. 8:15-16; 1 John 4:13). This testimony will usually be accompanied by a sense of being led by the Holy Spirit in paths of obedience to God's will (Rom. 8:14).*

2. *In addition, if the Holy Spirit is genuinely at work in our lives, he will be producing the kind of character traits that Paul calls "the fruit of the Spirit" (Gal. 5:22).*

3. *Related to this kind of fruit is another kind of fruit—the results of one's life and ministry as they have influence on others and on the church.* [Grudem then references Jesus' words from Matthew 7:16-20: "You will recognize them by their fruits...[17]...every healthy tree bears good fruit, but the diseased tree bears bad fruit. [18]A healthy tree cannot bear bad fruit, nor can a diseased tree bear good fruit...[20]Thus you will recognize them by their fruits."]

---

[4] Grudem, Wayne. *Systematic Theology: An Introduction to Biblical Doctrine.* (Grand Rapids, Mich.: Zondervan Publishing, 1994), 803.
[5] Ibid., 804.

4. *Another evidence of work of the Holy Spirit is continuing to believe and accept the sound teaching of the church.* [1 John 2:23-24, "No one who denies the Son has the Father...²⁴...If what you heard from the beginning abides in you, then you too will abide in the Son and in the Father" and also 1 John 4:6, "...Whoever knows God listens to us; whoever is not from God does not listen to us..."]

5. *Another evidence of genuine salvation is a continuing present relationship with Jesus Christ.* [John 15:4, 7, "Abide in me, and I in you...⁷If you abide in me, and my words abide in you, ask whatever you wish, and it will be done for you." Then, Grudem continues in his own words, "This abiding in Christ will include not only day-by-day trust in him in various situations, but also certainly regular fellowship with him in prayer and worship."]

6. *Finally, a major area of evidence that we are genuine believers is found in a life of obedience to God's commands.* [1 John 2:4-6, "Whoever says 'I know him' but does not keep his commandments is a liar, and the truth is not in him, ⁵but whoever keeps his word, in him truly the love of God is perfected. By this we may be sure that we are in him: ⁶whoever says he abides in him ought to walk in the same way in which he walked."]

Do I see a long-term pattern of growth in my Christian life?

The first two areas of assurance dealt with present faith and present evidence of the Holy Spirit at work in our lives. But Peter gives one more kind of test that we can use to ask whether we are genuinely believers. He tells us that there are some character traits which, if we keep on increasing in them, will guarantee that we will 'never fall' (2 Peter 1:10)...This implies that our assurance of salvation can be something that increases over time in our lives. Every year that we add to these character traits in our lives, we gain greater and greater assurance of our salvation. Thus, though young believers can have a quite strong confidence in their salvation, that assurance can increase to even deeper certainty over the years in which they grow toward Christian maturity.[6]

At this point, reviewing past experiences can help the student see a long-term pattern. Looking back to see God's work in his life can reinforce the assurance that "he who began a good work in you will bring it to completion at the day of Jesus Christ" (Philippians 1:6b). Encourage the student to talk about personal experiences that he has had with the Lord.

> "…though young believers can have a quite strong confidence in their salvation, that assurance can increase to even deeper certainty over the years in which they grow toward Christian maturity."
>
> —WAYNE GRUDEM

Look for ways in which faith was personalized or became "real" to the student. You may recall moments in early childhood when he seemed especially responsive to the Lord. Talk about these times and encourage him in this. You may even want to pause and rejoice in the Lord's kindness and grace, giving thanks for making Himself known.

Consider giving the student an assignment to interview one or two people who have known him long enough to see evidence of faith in his life. This can be an encouraging experience, and it can provide another way to reveal a pattern of spiritual growth and development.

As you come to the end of this session, you or the student may not see sufficient evidence of saving faith. Perhaps there are areas of rebellion, disobedience against God, and/or unbelief that have surfaced in your discussions. If this is the case, encourage the student to pray and spend time seeking the Lord

---

[6] Grudem, Wayne. *Systematic Theology: An Introduction to Biblical Doctrine*. (Grand Rapids, Mich.: Zondervan Publishing, 1994), 805.

in His Word. Working through the next two steps will help you decide if you should proceed, or if you should wait until there is more evidence and assurance of saving faith.

Make sure you earnestly pray and intercede for the student. In Genesis 25, Isaac prayed to the Lord for a child to be born to Rebekah and "the Lord granted his prayer" (verse 21). How much more will the Lord hear our prayer when we ask Him to reveal Himself to our children? I believe and have found it to be true in my own parenting experience that the Lord loves to answer that kind of prayer. Let's rely on Him to answer our prayers!

Step 4: Affirmation of Faith

4.1 Goal

This session is intended to provide the student with an opportunity to consciously and solemnly express his trust in and allegiance to Christ, thus exalting the regenerating power of the gospel over his will. If the student is preparing for baptism, this session provides a safe place for him to freely respond to questions similar to those he will be asked at his baptism. If the student does not feel ready to answer "yes" to these questions, he is more likely to respond truthfully in the privacy of your meetings than he would if he were standing up to his waist in water and surrounded by a crowd of people.

4.2 Personal Accountability to God

Help the student understand that each of us must respond to God personally and individually. The student will stand before an infinitely righteous Judge one day and will have to give an account for the life he lived. Have the student read the following texts and describe in his own words what the text is teaching.

> *Romans 14:10—Why do you pass judgment on your brother? Or you, why do you despise your brother? For* **we will all stand before the judgment seat of God;**

> *Revelation 20:11-15—Then I saw a great white throne and him who was seated on it. From his presence earth and sky fled away, and no place was found for them. [12]And I saw the dead, great and small,* **standing before the throne**, *and books were opened. Then another book was opened, which is the book of life. And the dead were judged by what was written in the books, according to what they had done. [13]And the sea gave up the dead who were in it, Death and Hades gave up the dead who were in them, and they were judged, each one of them, according to what they had done. [14]Then Death and*

> *Hades were thrown into the lake of fire. This is the second death, the lake of fire. ¹⁵And if anyone's name was not found written in the book of life, he was thrown into the lake of fire.*

Remind the student that his hope at the judgment will rest not in the church he attended or the faith of his parents, but on whether he is trusting and treasuring Christ.

4.3 Affirmation of Faith

Explore several Bible texts about when people had an opportunity to express their intention to follow Jesus.

> *Matthew 4:19—And he said to them, "Follow me, and I will make you fishers of men."*
>
> *Matthew 8:21-22—Another of the disciples said to him, "Lord, let me first go and bury my father." ²²And Jesus said to him, "Follow me, and leave the dead to bury their own dead."*
>
> *Matthew 9:9—As Jesus passed on from there, he saw a man called Matthew sitting at the tax booth, and he said to him, "Follow me." And he rose and followed him.*
>
> *Matthew 16:24—Then Jesus told his disciples, "If anyone would come after me, let him deny himself and take up his cross and follow me."*
>
> *Matthew 19:21—Jesus said to him, "If you would be perfect, go, sell what you possess and give to the poor, and you will have treasure in heaven; and come, follow me."*

Review the following three questions that affirm faith in Christ.

Question #1

Are you now trusting in Jesus Christ alone for the forgiveness of your sins and for the fulfillment of all His promises to you, even eternal life?

- Reinforce that this question affirms a present trust in Christ—"Are you now trusting..." See section 3.3 where we discussed that a present trust in Jesus is one of the evidences of genuine faith ("Do I have a present trust in Christ for salvation?").
- Reinforce what he is trusting Christ for.
- Reinforce the word "alone" since "there is salvation in no one else, for there is no other name under heaven given among men by which we must be saved" (Acts 4:12).

> **"And there is salvation in no one else, for there is no other name under heaven given among men by which we must be saved."**
>
> —ACTS 4:12

Question #2

Do you renounce Satan in all his works and all his ways?

Make sure the student understands what it means to "renounce Satan." It may be helpful to explain that when a person wants to become a citizen of another country he must renounce all loyalty and allegiance to his native country. Our response to this question affirms that we now belong to Jesus. We honor Him as our King and renounce all allegiance to Satan and his work and his ways.

Question #3

Do you intend, with God's help, to obey Jesus' teachings and to follow Him as your Lord?

The aim of this question is to affirm the student's intention to obey and follow Christ, recognizing that apart from Him and His grace we can do nothing, including obeying and following Him. Like the first question, this is really expressing our trust in Christ.

The student responds.

- When you are ready, make eye contact with the student and solemnly ask him:

  1. *Are you now trusting in Jesus Christ alone for the forgiveness of your sins and for the fulfillment of all His promises to you, even eternal life?*
     (Student responds, "I am.")

  2. *Do you renounce Satan in all his works and all his ways?*
     (Student responds, "I do.")

  3. *Do you intend, with God's help, to obey Jesus' teachings and to follow Him as your Lord?*
     (Student responds, "I do.")

- Encourage the student to pray and express his resolve to follow the Lord.

  Example: *Dear Jesus, now that I am older and have heard the gospel again, I understand better the seriousness of my sin. I still desire to turn away from my sin and trust You for forgiveness and to follow You wherever You lead me.*

- At this point, you might want to document the student's response by recording it on a certificate or in a Bible.

  Example: *On this day, [date], after my [Parent/Mentor] reviewed the gospel with me again, I declare that I am trusting Jesus for the forgiveness of my sins and for the hope of eternal life. It is my sincere desire to follow Him in obedience all the days of my life.*

Step 5: The Meaning of Baptism

5.1 Goal

The goal of this session is to help the student understand the meaning and significance of baptism. This is especially helpful if the student is preparing to be baptized. If he has already been baptized, I still recommend working through this step. Many young people (and some adults) who have been baptized do not fully understand what it is, why we practice it, and what it means.

5.2 What is baptism?

Begin by asking what the student already understands about baptism. Affirm what he knows already, and then fill in whatever gaps there are in his understanding.

Immersion into Water

This is the basic meaning of the word "baptism," but for the Christian its meaning is much richer and deeper.

Baptism is a symbol.

The Death and Resurrection of Jesus

The pool of water in baptism beautifully illustrates this point. If we think of the pool as a grave, we descend with Christ into the grave and die to our sin. In Christ, death has no power to hold us in the grave. Because Jesus rose from the dead, we rise with Him, free from the power of sin and death, to life everlasting.

> *1 Corinthians 15:1-4—Now I would remind you, brothers, of the gospel I preached to you, which you received, in which you stand, ²and by which you are being saved, if you hold fast to the word I preached to you—unless you believed in*

> vain. *³For I delivered to you as of first importance what I also received: that Christ died for our sins in accordance with the Scriptures, ⁴that he was buried, that he was raised on the third day in accordance with the Scriptures,*

What God Has Accomplished

Baptism is a symbol of the spiritual change that God has worked in our lives. This spiritual change is a transition from spiritual and eternal death to spiritual and eternal life. It is moving from hopelessness into hopefulness, darkness into light, and slavery to sin into freedom in Christ. In baptism, we symbolically express our acceptance of death with Christ, putting an end to our old way of life and rising with Christ to begin a new kind of life in Him.

> *Romans 6:3-11—Do you not know that all of us who have been baptized into Christ Jesus were baptized into his death? ⁴We were buried therefore with him by baptism into death, in order that, just as Christ was raised from the dead by the glory of the Father, we too might walk in newness of life. ⁵For if we have been united with him in a death like his, we shall certainly be united with him in a resurrection like his. ⁶We know that our old self was crucified with him in order that the body of sin might be brought to nothing, so that we would no longer be enslaved to sin. ⁷For one who has died has been set free from sin. ⁸Now if we have died with Christ, we believe that we will also live with him. ⁹We know that Christ, being raised from the dead will never die again; death no longer has dominion over him. ¹⁰For the death he died he died to sin, once for all, but the life he lives he lives to God. ¹¹So you also must consider yourselves dead to sin and alive to God in Christ Jesus.*

> *Colossians 2:9-14—For in him the whole fullness of deity dwells bodily, ¹⁰and you have been filled in him, who is the head of all rule and authority. ¹¹In him also you were circumcised with a circumcision made without hands,*

> by putting off the body of the flesh, by the circumcision of Christ, ¹²having been buried with him in baptism, in which you were also raised with him through faith in the powerful working of God, who raised him from the dead. ¹³And you, who were dead in your trespasses and the uncircumcision of your flesh, God made alive together with him, having forgiven us all our trespasses, ¹⁴by canceling the record of debt that stood against us with its legal demands. This he set aside, nailing it to the cross.

Washing/Cleansing from Sin

> Titus 3:5—he saved us, not because of works done by us in righteousness, but according to his own mercy, by the washing of regeneration and renewal of the Holy Spirit,

> Acts 22:16—"And now why do you wait? Rise and be baptized and wash away your sins, calling on his name."

Entrance into the Body of Christ, the Church

> 1 Corinthians 12:12-13—For just as the body is one and has many members, and all the members of the body, though many, are one body, so it is with Christ. ¹³For in one Spirit we were all baptized into one body—Jews or Greeks, slaves or free—and all were made to drink of one Spirit.

Explain to the student that this is why baptism usually occurs at a public service in the context of the local church, and this is why baptism is often connected with church membership.

Baptism is an act of obedience to the Lord's command and following His example.

> Matthew 28:18-20—And Jesus came and said to them, "All authority in heaven and on earth has been given to me. ¹⁹Go therefore and make disciples of all nations, baptizing them in the name of the Father and of the Son and of the Holy Spirit, ²⁰teaching them to observe all

> *that I have commanded you. And behold, I am with you always, to the end of the age."*

> *Acts 2:38—And Peter said to them, "Repent and be baptized every one of you in the name of Jesus Christ for the forgiveness of your sins, and you will receive the gift of the Holy Spirit."*

> *Matthew 3:13-17—Then Jesus came from Galilee to the Jordan to John, to be baptized by him. ¹⁴John would have prevented him, saying, "I need to be baptized by you, and do you come to me?" ¹⁵But Jesus answered him, "Let it be so now, for thus it is fitting for us to fulfill all righteousness." Then he consented. ¹⁶And when Jesus was baptized, immediately he went up from the water, and behold, the heavens were opened to him, and he saw the Spirit of God descending like a dove and coming to rest on him; ¹⁷and behold, a voice from heaven said, "This is my beloved Son, with whom I am well pleased."*

Baptism is a public declaration of faith in Jesus Christ.

In baptism, we express with our whole body our heart's acceptance of Christ's lordship. Becoming a Christian involves the body as well as the heart. In conversion, the heart is freed from slavery to sin to be enslaved to God.

> *Romans 6:12-13—Let not sin therefore reign in your mortal body, to make you obey its passions. ¹³Do not present your members to sin as instruments for unrighteousness, but present yourselves to God as those who have been brought from death to life, and your members to God as instruments for righteousness.*

Explain that since the lordship of Christ lays claim to our whole body, it is fitting for us to express our surrender to His lordship with our whole body.

Baptism gives expression that we are God's from head to toe.[7]

Baptism is a blessing.

The student should understand by now that baptism does not accomplish our salvation, but he should not miss the great blessing in the baptism experience. Wayne Grudem captures the beauty of this blessing:

> *In all the discussion over the mode of baptism and the disputes over its meaning, it is easy for Christians to lose sight of the significance and beauty of baptism and to disregard the tremendous blessing that accompanies this ceremony. The amazing truths of passing through the waters of judgment safely, of dying and rising with Christ, and of having our sins washed away, are truths of momentous and eternal proportion and ought to be an occasion for giving great glory and praise to God. If churches would teach these truths more clearly, baptisms would be the occasion of much more blessing in the church.*[8]

> "...it is easy for Christians to lose sight of the significance and beauty of baptism and to disregard the tremendous blessing that accompanies this ceremony."
> —WAYNE GRUDEM

Baptism is only for believers.

Since baptism is a symbol of beginning the Christian life, we should only baptize when there is evidence of new birth and the student is able to give a credible profession of faith in Christ.

---

[7] This insight came from an evening baptism meditation by Pastor John Piper of Bethlehem Baptist Church of Minneapolis, Minnesota on September 28, 1980.
[8] Grudem, Wayne. *Systematic Theology: an Introduction to Biblical Doctrine.* (Grand Rapids, Mich: Zondervan Publishing, 1994), 969.

Step 6: Preparing a Testimony

6.1 Goal

This step is intended to help the student put words to his experience and express his faith in a way that will glorify God, encourage others, and point people to Christ for years to come. Taking the time to work through this step is especially important if the student is being prepared for baptism, since he will likely have one or more opportunities to share his testimony.

6.2 The Intimidation Factor

The idea of giving his testimony can feel intimidating to a student anticipating baptism. In some cases, this fear is enough to keep him from following through with baptism.

We should do all we can to encourage the student in his faith, while recognizing that a measure of apprehension and concern about this is good. This is an opportunity to remind him that when we follow Jesus, He leads us "in paths of righteousness" (Psalm 23:3), but those paths are not always easy. The concern a student may have about giving his testimony provides an opportunity for him to learn how to look to Jesus for the courage and grace he will need to follow Him. This may bring some to the place where they must count the cost of following the Lord.

6.3 A "Credible" Profession of Faith

Before baptizing someone, church leaders often require at least one meeting with a candidate to confirm that he is ready to be baptized. The candidate's testimony can be very helpful to church leadership for discerning a credible profession of faith.

A credible testimony has both objective and subjective reality to it. Objectively, the testimony should reflect an understanding of the gospel and the meaning of baptism. Subjectively, the testimony should communicate that the student is born again. Is this real for him, or is he just parroting what he has been taught to say? Does the gospel seem precious to him? Does he manifest genuine affection for Jesus? Is the grace of God "amazing" to him?

6.4 Preparing the "Objective" Part of the Testimony

Preparing the student to communicate objectively will be relatively easy if he was tracking with you in the preceding sessions, especially steps two and five. Keep in mind that in his testimony the student should answer the following questions:

> "Is this real for him, or is he just parroting what he has been taught to say? Does the gospel seem precious to him? Does he manifest genuine affection for Jesus? Is the grace of God 'amazing' to him?"
>
> —DAVID MICHAEL

1. *What was the problem?— Why did I need salvation? (with supporting Scripture)*

2. *What did God do through Christ to solve that problem? (with supporting Scripture)*

3. *How do I benefit from what Christ did? (with supporting Scripture)*

4. *How did God bring me to the point where I was willing to obtain this benefit?*

Even though the student does not need to provide an exhaustive treatment of the doctrine of salvation, he should be able to say one or two things in response to each question to reflect a basic understanding of these glorious truths.

The fourth question is often where testimonies begin and end. It is encouraging for people to hear (and tell) the story of how Jesus became precious and the changes He wrought in our lives. Young people growing up in Christian homes can sometimes feel like there is not much to say here. Many will say "I grew up in a Christian home where my parents introduced me to Jesus when I was young, and I have been trusting Him ever since."

Remind the student that if this is his story, it is no small blessing to be given godly parents who treasure Christ. Millions of people have been born into godless families where they have been cut off from the truth and have made a ruin of their lives. Consider with him the providence of God in bringing him into a Christian home. Encourage him to consider how God worked to bring his parents to faith in Christ, and perhaps their parents before them. You could ask, "What if your parents had never known the Lord? What if your parents had never known each other?"

Also remind the student that, according to Ephesians 1:3-4, God's saving work in his life began before the world began.

> *Ephesians 1:3-4—Blessed be the God and Father of our Lord Jesus Christ, who has blessed us in Christ with every spiritual blessing in the heavenly places, ⁴even as he chose us in him before the foundation of the world, that we should be holy and blameless before him…*

6.5 Preparing the "Subjective" Part of the Testimony

In preparing to communicate the objective part of the testimony, it is often helpful for the student to write down what he wants to say. However, when it comes to communicating his heart for the truth, his love for Christ, and the preciousness of the gospel, a written document can often be a hindrance. The following are some ideas for how to help the student with this.

- When preparing his testimony, even if he writes it down, encourage him to express his thoughts in his own words.
- Writing out his testimony can help him organize his thoughts, but once he has done this, encourage him to try sharing his testimony without the manuscript. Fewer, imprecise words coming from the heart are often more meaningful to the listeners than well-structured, well-articulated thoughts that are read from a prepared statement.
- Encourage the student to keep his focus on the opportunity his testimony provides to glorify God and to proclaim the gospel.
- Help the student shift his attention away from himself and consider those who will be listening to what he has to say. Give him a vision for how the Lord might be pleased to use his testimony to bless others. How might the Lord bless those who will hear him speak? Perhaps the Lord will be pleased to use him to encourage other believers in their faith. Perhaps there will be parents in the audience who are concerned about an unbelieving child. Perhaps the Lord will use his testimony to fuel their prayers and keep them trusting the Lord for their children. There are almost always unbelieving friends and family members present when young people are being baptized. Perhaps the Lord will use this testimony to open their eyes to the beauty of Christ and glory of the gospel (which, by the way, is another good reason for including the gospel in our testimonies). Pray about these possibilities and invite others to pray with you and the student as the testimony is being prepared.
- Encourage the student to rest in the confidence that the Holy Spirit is the one who "bears witness" in our testimony "that we are children of God" (Romans 8:16).

The Ordinance of Baptism

Jesus established two ordinances to be practiced by the church—baptism and the Lord's Supper. The church leadership is charged with overseeing and conducting these ordinances in a manner that is biblical and pleasing to the Lord. When a church practices "believer's baptism," a person must have a publicly credible faith before he is baptized and admitted into membership. Recognizing that only God can perfectly discern the affections of the heart, the steps in this process are designed to help parents and church leaders discern the credibility of the student's faith.

When Should a Young Person Be Baptized?

There are differences among those who embrace believer's baptism concerning the timing of baptism for children who profess faith in Christ. Some argue for "immediate participation," meaning that children should be baptized as soon as they can confess faith in Christ. My approach to preparing young people for baptism over the years has been more aligned with the "withholding" view that encourages children to wait until there is sufficient maturity, understanding, and evidence of genuine faith. The specific reasons I have given to parents can be found in Appendix II. More important than the age of the child is the evidence of regeneration and sufficient maturity to articulate the gospel and give a credible profession of faith.

Appendix I

Two Views on Childhood Participation in Church Ordinances

by Scott Holman and Jared Kennedy[9]
Sojourn Community Church, Louisville, Kentucky

There are two positions within the Baptist tradition regarding the questions of childhood participation in the church ordinances, baptism and communion, and childhood church membership. The two views are:

1. Withholding baptism and communion from children until they reach a level of maturity that is independent of their parents in matters relating to God and the church.
2. Immediate participation in baptism and communion for believing children, who are recognized as church members with limited responsibilities.

Early in the church's history, some began wrongly baptizing infants. This was in spite of the fact that the church during the New Testament times had only baptized believers—baptizing only after evidence of a changed heart. Infant children were considered to be part of "covenant families"—children of Christians to whom God had promised a family inheritance. Families who baptize their infant children expect that God will confirm this promise by giving faith to their children as they grow to adulthood. In churches that practice infant baptism, a child's faith is often "confirmed"—sometimes with a special ceremony—once the child has reached an age of accountability. The Baptist tradition, though only several hundred years old,

---

[9] Our thanks to Scott Holman and Jared Kennedy for giving us permission to include this paper with our material. This paper is part of a booklet which they published entitled *Childhood Baptism and Church Membership: A Position and Policy for Sojourn Community Church*. When they were developing this booklet for their church, they requested permission to use some of the ideas and wording from our material.

has always practiced *believer's baptism*, rejecting the infant baptism of the Catholic, Lutheran, Anglican, and Reformed traditions.

Both positions on childhood participation in church ordinances have strong historical support. In 1858, Southern Baptist theologian, John Dagg, wrote in favor of immediate participation for children:

> *Intelligent piety has, in all ages, been found in children who have not yet reached maturity; and such children have a Scriptural right to church-membership [which would imply participation in baptism and communion].*[10]

In 1864, Charles Spurgeon, an English Baptist pastor who wrote extensively about teaching the gospel to children, preached a sermon, in which he seems to imply that his Metropolitan Tabernacle also welcomed children as members:

> *Of the many boys and girls whom we have received into Church-fellowship, I can say of them all, they have gladdened my heart, and I have never received any with greater confidence than I have these.*[11]

On the other hand, it is worth noting—if only as an historical point—that most Baptists in history were not baptized until their late teens or early twenties. Most held jobs before they were baptized. Even Spurgeon waited to baptize his own sons—who may have been believers for years—until they were eighteen.[12] Simply put, as far as Baptists were concerned, baptizing young children was rare.

This is not the case in Southern Baptist churches today.

---

[10] Dagg, John L. "Chapter 4: Infant Church Membership" in *Manual of Theology, Second Part: A Treatise on Church Order*. (Greenville, South Carolina: The Southern Baptist Publication Society, 1858), available at www.founders.org/library/dagg_vol2/ch4.html.

[11] Spurgeon, Charles H. "Children Brought to Christ, and Not to the Font [of Infant Baptism]." A sermon at the Metropolitan Tabernacle, Newington, on Sunday, July 24, 1864; available at The Spurgeon Archive, www.spurgeon.org/sermons/0581.htm.

[12] Dever, Mark E. "Baptism in the Context of the Local Church" in Believer's Baptism: Sign of the New Covenant in Christ, ed. Thomas R. Schreiner and Shawn D. Wright, (Nashville: Broadman & Holman, 2006), 346. Also see W. Y. Fullerton's, *Thomas Spurgeon: A Biography*. (London: Hodder & Stoughton, 1919), 43-45.

Between 1977 and 1997 there was a 250 percent increase in the number of baptisms of children under age six in Southern Baptist churches.[13] Moreover, there is evidence that this trend is not only recent but distinctly American. English Baptist Anthony Cross observes that Southern Baptists tend to approve of baptizing younger persons than do Baptists in England.[14] Why is this the case?

Perhaps our parental desire to see our children saved has trumped our responsibility as both parents and church members to protect our children and the church from error. We want to see our children embrace Christ and experience authentic salvation. This is right and good, but it can nevertheless be dangerous if we are not equally wary of deceiving our children by giving false assurances. In our day, there is a tremendous amount of social pressure on the church's pastoral leadership to confirm the conversion of a young child.[15] Pastors and teachers must take care not to pressure children for a quick decision without waiting for understanding about what it means to turn away from sin and truly trust in Jesus. Parents also should consider how dangerous it is for the church to allow nominal Christians—those who are believers in name only— into its membership. Nominal Christians weaken the church by giving a false witness to the watching world, and pose even greater dangers if given positions as teachers or leaders. In the 1840s, J. L. Reynolds issued the following warning:

> *The recognition of unconverted persons, as members of a Christian Church, is an evil of no ordinary magnitude. It throws down the wall of partition which Christ himself has erected and obliterates the distinction between the church and the world...An accession of nominal Christians may enlarge its numbers, but cannot augment its real strength.*

---

[13] Hemphil, Tony. "The Practice of Infantile Baptism in Southern Baptist Churches and Subsequent Impact on Regenerate Church Membership," *Faith & Mission 18.3.* (Summer 2001): 74-87.

[14] Cross, Anthony. *Baptism and the Baptists: Theology and Practice in Twentieth Century Britain.* (Carslisle, United Kingdom: Paternoster, 2000), 393 n. 23. (Cross gives English Baptist examples of churches accepting children ages 8-12, but observes that English Baptists rarely accept preschool age children for baptism.)

[15] John Withers, "Social Forces Affecting the Age at Which Children are Baptized in Southern Baptist Churches," Ph.D. diss., The Southern Baptist Theological Seminary, 1996.

> *A Church that welcomes to the privileges of Christ's house, the unconverted, under the specious pretext of increasing the number of his followers, in reality betrays the citadel to his foes.*[16]

So, the issue of childhood baptism and church membership is important on at least two levels. First, it has to do with our children, for whom we desire salvation. Second, because it involves the ordinances (baptism and communion), it has to do with the visible witness of the church in the world.

Position #1: Withholding

The arguments for withholding baptism and communion from children until they reach a level of maturity that is independent of their parents in matters relating to God and the church are as follows:[17]

1. Children, just like adults, are sinful, and they are in need of Jesus' saving work (Psalm 51:5; Romans 5:12-21).

2. Children can be saved. Christ invites children to come to him (1 Samuel 1-3; Psalm 22:9-10; 1 Kings 18:12; 2 Kings 22; 2 Chronicles 34:35; Jeremiah 1:5-8; Luke 1:15; Luke 18:16), and he uses children as examples of the humility necessary for those who wish to enter Jesus' kingdom (Matthew 11:25; Matthew 18:2-4; Matthew 19:13-14; Mark 10:15-16; Luke 10:21; Luke 18:14-16).

---

[16] Reynolds, J.L. *Church Polity or the Kingdom of Christ (1849), in Polity.* Edited by M.E. Dever. (Washington, D.C.: Center for Church Reform, 2001), 327.

[17] See Jim Butler's "Church Membership and Young Children" a paper presented to Free Grace Baptist Church of Chilliwack, British Columbia on April 14, 2001; Mark E. Dever's "Baptism in the Context," pages 344-350; "The Baptism of Children at Capitol Hill Baptist Church," a paper presented to Capitol Hill Baptist Church of Washington, D.C. in 2004; "Who Should Be Baptized? At What Age Should Believers Be Baptized?" a sermon at Capitol Hill Baptist Church, Washington, D.C., on Sunday, April 21, 2002; Jim Elliff's "How Children Come to Faith in Christ," audiocassettes, (Little Rock, Ark.: Family Life, 1994), [MP3s are available from Christian Communicators Online at www.ccwonline.org.]; "Childhood Conversion," available at Christian Communicators Online at www.ccwonline.org/cconv.html; Jim Elliff and Daryl Wingerd's "Is Baptism a Requirement of Church Membership?" available at Christian Communicators Online, www.ccwonline.org/baptismrq.html; and David W. Merck's "Children and Church Membership," available at The Reformed Reader, www.reformedreader.org/rbs/cacm.htm

3. Baptism and communion should be given immediately when one's confession of faith is publicly credible. For adults, this means living in the community of faith for a time and being examined by the elders and larger community who watch for an authentic trust in Christ that is independent of others.

4. It is not clear in the New Testament that children were ever baptized or that we should expect they should be (e.g., Acts 4:4, 32; Acts 5:6, Acts 12:14; Acts 6:1; Acts 8:1-3, 12; Acts 9:2; Acts 10:24, 33, 44-48; Acts 12:13). All followers of Christ described in the New Testament are baptized as adults, who are actively participating in church life.

5. A child's faith is primarily nurtured by his or her parents (Ephesians 6:4)—primarily the father, who provides pastoral direction to his child. The New Testament teaching that children must obey their parents (Ephesians 6:1; Colossians 3:20) implies that children relate to God and the church primarily through their parents, and they are not on independent standing before God (see also 1 Corinthians 7:14).

6. Moreover, children are easily deceived. They require the constant supervision and care of parental authority (Proverbs 22:15; Ephesians 4:14-15; 1 Corinthians 13:11).

7. Due to immaturity, children have had little chance to express their trust in Christ independently from their parents. For example, they have had few opportunities to choose between Christ and their peers in a deep way. They cannot make a publicly credible confession.

8. Therefore, baptism and communion should be withheld from children until they reach a level of maturity that is independent of their parents.

9. Moreover, baptism and communion are inseparable from active membership and participation in the local church. So, children should be excluded from church membership as well.

10. God's saving grace is not given through baptism and communion. So, there is no danger to the child in waiting. In fact, waiting can increase the honor associated with this event, as well as allow time for the child's discipline and faith to grow.

"Withholding" at its Worst

In its attempt to judge the faithfulness of each individual's testimony by the fruits of that person's life (Matthew 7:16; 1 John 4:1ff; James 2), the church begins to emphasize good works as a means of self-assessment. Tender children (and adults), in whom the Spirit is at work, may be discouraged by their continuing sinfulness and lack of apparent fruit. A well-intentioned policy may become a stumbling block that encourages these children to have a fearful and introspective view of their spiritual lives. Parents may be discouraged as well, and "withholding" could become an excuse for them to lower their expectations and put off training their children in spiritual things. The adolescent period may be prolonged and filled with many failures. If this occurs, God will judge the church's teachers for being stumbling blocks to the little ones in their care (Matthew 18:6).

"Withholding" at its Best

The church welcomes young adults into its membership with the confidence that they have demonstrated evidence of change and new life throughout their adolescent years. These young people demonstrate a deep understanding of the Christian faith without confusion, and they gladly look forward to their public confession and baptism. Once joining the church, these adult believers have fond memories of their baptism as a significant event and rite of passage. In the process, the church's reputation and leadership is protected from those who are Christians in name only.

Resources for Parents

Dever, Mark E. "Who Should Be Baptized? At What Age Should Believers Be Baptized?" Sermon at the Capitol Hill Baptist Church, Washington, D.C., on Sunday, April 21, 2002.

Elliff, Jim. *How Children Come to Faith in Christ.* Audio cassettes. (Little Rock, AR: Family Life, 1994.) MP3s available at Christian Communicators Online, www.ccwonline.org.

Romero, Daniel. "Childhood Conversion." Christian Communicators Online, www.ccwonline.org/cconv.html.

Position #2: Immediate Participation

The arguments for immediate participation in baptism and communion for believing children who are also recognized as church members with limited responsibilities are as follows:[18]

1. Children, just like adults, are sinful, and they are in need of Jesus' saving work (Psalm 51:5; Romans 5:12-21).

2. Children can be saved. Christ invites children to come to him (1 Samuel 1-3; Psalm 22:9-10; 1 Kings 18:12; 2 Kings 22; 2 Chronicles 3435; Jeremiah 1:5-8; Luke 1:15; Luke 18:16), and he uses children as examples of the humility necessary for those who wish to enter Jesus' kingdom (Matthew 11:25; Matthew 18:2-4; Matthew 19:13-14; Mark 10:15-16; Luke 10:21; Luke 18:14-16).

3. Believing children should be welcomed into the church through baptism. The NT authors addressed these children as members within the church (Ephesians 6:1 "in the Lord;" Colossians 3:20), and we should as well.

---

[18] See: Ted Christ's *Forbid Them Not: Rethinking the Baptism and Church Membership of Children and Young People.* (Owensboro, Kent.: Heritage Baptist Church); John L. Dagg's "Chapter 4: Infant Church Membership" in *Manual of Theology, Second Part: A Treatise on Church Order.* (Greenville, South Carol.: The Southern Baptist Publication Society, 1858); text found at www.founders.org/library/dagg_vol2/ch4.html; Charles H. Spurgeon's "Children Brought to Christ, and Not to the Font," a sermon at the Metropolitan Tabernacle, Newington on Sunday, July 24, 1864. (Available at The Spurgeon Archive, www.spurgeon.org/sermons/0581.htm)

4. The New Testament knows nothing of un-baptized followers of Christ. If a child is a believer, he or she is a disciple. If a child is a disciple, then Christ commands that this child participate in baptism and communion (Matthew 28:18-10).

5. Baptism and communion are intended for every member of Christ's church. They are ways of experiencing and remembering God's goodness and the gracious gifts that he has lavished on his people. None of Jesus' gracious gifts—worship, teaching, preaching, community, pastoral care, communion, or even church discipline—should be withheld from young followers of Christ.

6. In his pastoral epistles, Paul limits the position of elder to men (1 Timothy 2:11-12; 3:2). Moreover, the term "elder" itself suggests that the attainment of age and experience is required for one to exercise this role in the church (though Timothy should not be considered to be too young—1 Timothy 4:12). Paul also sets an age limit (age 60) for widows who can receive support from the church (1 Timothy 5:9). In the spirit of these limitations, it is suggested that church leadership roles and responsibilities that call for a certain level of maturity should be withheld from children until they reach that level. In other words, believing children are full-fledged members of the church that have limited responsibilities until they reach a level of independence from their parents. Until that time, their primary responsibility *in the Lord* is to obey their parents (Ephesians 6:1).

"Immediate Participation" at its Worst

The social pressure on the church's leadership may lead them to confirm the salvation of children at a very young age. Teachers and parents may pressure children for quick decisions without waiting for understanding about what it means to turn away from sins and truly trust in Jesus. False assurances may be given to some children. As these children grow, their Christianity is shown to lack credibility, and this damages the church's public reputation as well as its witness to the gospel. As loving shepherds of the church, the elders are responsible to confront any professed believer (adult or child) whose life is not lived in accord with his confession (2 Timothy 4:1-5; Hebrews 13:17). Therefore, if a baptized child continues in sin without repenting, the elders will have to take corrective measures. The goal in any "church discipline" situation is restoration, and our hope is that any correction from [Sojourn Church's] elders would augment parents' discipline. The worst case scenario would occur if the elders were at odds with the parents.

"Immediate Participation" at its Best

The church teaches parents that salvation is a work of God and not merely a decision by the believer. Children, like adults, show understanding and evidence of believing faith before the church accepts them for baptism. Christ's goodness, love, and gracious mercy are taught to children. The church receives believing children into its membership and corporate worship gatherings with confidence and glad hearts—knowing that their faith is made strong by Christ. The children, encouraged to obey their parents, read their Bibles, and talk to God in prayer, grow in wisdom and grace even as they grow in stature.

Resources for Parents

Christman, Ted. *Forbid Them Not: Rethinking the Baptism and Church Membership of Children and Young People.* (Owensboro, Kent.: Heritage Baptist Church).

Spurgeon, Charles H. "Children Brought to Christ, and Not to the Font." Sermon delivered at the Metropolitan Tabernacle, Newington on Sunday, July 24, 1864. Available at The Spurgeon Archive, www.spurgeon.org/sermons/0581.htm.

Appendix II

Concerning the Age of Baptism for Children: Reasons for Waiting

by Pastor David Michael

Over my years of ministry, I have encouraged parents to wait until their children are at least 11 years old before being baptized. The Bible does not give us a precise age at which we should baptize children. All that we can legitimately infer from biblical teaching on baptism is that a child must be able to give a credible profession of faith. I believe that there are many younger children who could make such a profession but may not be ready for baptism. I also believe that there are older children who could give a "credible" profession but may not be ready for baptism.

Reasons for Waiting

My reasons for encouraging young people to wait until at least age 11 are driven mainly by a larger discipleship strategy for young people. By holding off until this age or later, we can maximize the spiritual benefit that the baptism experience will have for them. Here are some reasons for parents to consider before deciding when their children should begin preparing for baptism:

1. Baptism can be a very meaningful experience, and we want it to be one that a person remembers. The older a child is, the more likely he will remember and cherish the experience. If they are older when they are baptized, people are more likely to look back on this experience with the confidence that it reflected a conscious and sincere resolve to follow the Lord.

2. Even though a child may be able to articulate a basic understanding of the gospel and express a genuine desire to trust Christ, there needs to be sufficient time for his faith to

be tested, for others to witness the fruit of repentance, and for his understanding of the gospel to mature.

3. For a young person to wait and anticipate an experience is important and rare in a "me-oriented" culture that continually tells us, "If you want it, you can have it and you can have it now." Waiting for something precious and meaningful helps to make the experience more precious and meaningful when it arrives.

4. The promises that a person makes in baptism are weighty, and thus should not be made lightly. "If anyone would come after me, let him deny himself and take up his cross and follow me" (Mark 8:34b). We do not believe a younger child has the maturity or understanding to sufficiently count the cost of following Jesus.

5. Waiting until a child is older allows for more robust and thorough preparation for baptism. The preparation I recommend for young people can be an intellectual stretch for most 11-year-olds, and thus would require substantial simplification for younger children.

6. This preparation process is designed to help strengthen, deepen, and in some cases establish the young person's relationship with the spiritual leader in his life. A strategic time for the parent or mentor to establish a regular pattern of connecting and communication concerning matters of the heart and of faith is just before the young person enters the teen years.

> **"Even though a child may be able to articulate a basic understanding of the gospel and express a genuine desire to trust Christ, there needs to be sufficient time for his faith to be tested, for others to witness the fruit of repentance, and for his understanding of the gospel to mature."**
>
> —DAVID MICHAEL

Appendix III

What Can Give a Believer Genuine Assurance?

by Wayne Grudem[19]

If it is true...that those who are unbelievers and who finally fall away may give many external signs of conversion, then what will serve as evidence of genuine conversion? What can give real assurance to a real believer? We can list three categories of questions that a person could ask of himself or herself.

1. Do I Have a Present Trust in Christ for Salvation?

> Paul tells the Colossians that they will be saved on the last day, "provided that you *continue in the faith* stable and steadfast, not shifting from the hope of the gospel which you heard" (Col. 1:23, [RSV]). The author of Hebrews says, "We share in Christ, if only we hold our first confidence firm to the end" (Heb. 3:14) and encourages his readers to be imitators of those "who *through faith* and patience inherit the promises" (Heb. 6:12). In fact, the most famous verse in the entire Bible uses a present tense verb that may be translated, "whoever continues believing in him" may have eternal life (see John 3:16).
>
> Therefore a person should ask himself or herself, "Do I today have trust in Christ to forgive my sins and take me without blame into heaven forever? Do I have confidence in my heart that he has saved me? If I were to die tonight and stand before God's judgment seat, and if he were to ask me why he should let me into heaven, would I begin to think of my good deeds and depend on them, or would I without hesitation say that I am depending on the merits of Christ and am confident that he is a sufficient Savior?"

---

[19] Excerpt from Wayne Grudem's book, *Systematic Theology: An Introduction to Biblical Doctrine*. (Grand Rapids, Michigan: Zondervan Publishing, 1994), 803-806. Used by permission.

This emphasis on *present* faith in Christ stands in contrast to the practice of some church "testimonies" where people repeatedly recite details of a conversion experience that may have happened 20 or 30 years ago. If a testimony of saving faith is genuine, it should be a testimony of faith that is active this very day.

2. **Is There Evidence of a Regenerating Work of the Holy Spirit in My Heart?**

> "In addition, if the Holy Spirit is genuinely at work in our lives, he will be producing the kind of character traits that Paul calls the 'fruit of the Spirit' (Gal. 5:22)."
>
> —WAYNE GRUDEM

The evidence of the work of the Holy Spirit in our hearts comes in many different forms. Although we should not put confidence in the demonstration of miraculous works (Matt. 7:22), or long hours and years of work at some local church (which may simply be building with "wood, hay, straw" [in terms of 1 Cor. 3:12] to further one's own ego or power over others, or to attempt to earn merit with God), there are many other evidences of a real work of the Holy Spirit in one's heart.

First, there is a subjective testimony of the Holy Spirit within our hearts bearing witness that we are God's children (Rom. 8:15-16; 1 John 4:13). This testimony will usually be accompanied by a sense of being led by the Holy Spirit in paths of obedience to God's will (Rom. 8:14).

In addition, if the Holy Spirit is genuinely at work in our lives, he will be producing the kind of character traits that Paul calls "the fruit of the Spirit" (Gal. 5:22). He lists several attitudes and character traits that are produced by the Holy Spirit: "love, joy, peace, patience, kindness, goodness, faithfulness, gentleness, self-control" (Gal. 5:22-23). Of course, the question is not, "Do I perfectly exemplify all of these characteristics in my life?" but rather, "Are these things a general characteristic of my life? Do I sense these attitudes in my heart? Do others (especially those closest to me) see these traits exhibited in my life? Have I been growing in them over a period of years?" There is no suggestion in the New Testament that any non-Christian, any unregenerate person, can convincingly fake these character traits, especially for those who know the person most closely.

Related to this kind of fruit is another kind of fruit—the results of one's life and ministry as they have influence on others and on the church. There are some people who profess to be Christians but whose influence on others is to discourage them, to drag them down, to injure their faith, and to provoke controversy and divisiveness. The result of their life and ministry is not to build up others and to build up the church, but to tear it down. On the other hand, there are those who seem to edify others in every conversation, every prayer, and every work of ministry they put their hand to. Jesus said, regarding false prophets, "You will know them by their fruits...Every sound tree bears good fruit, but the bad tree bears evil fruit...Thus you will know them by their fruits" (Matt. 7:16-20).

Another evidence of work of the Holy Spirit is continuing to believe and accept the sound teaching of the church. Those who begin to deny major doctrines of the faith give serious negative indications concerning their salvation: "No one who denies the Son has the Father...If what you heard from the beginning abides in you, then you will abide in the Son and in the Father" (1 John 2:23-24). John also says, "Whoever knows God listens to us, and he who is not of God does not listen to us" (1 John 4:6). Since the New Testament writings are the current replacement for the apostles like John, we might also say that whoever knows God will continue to read and to delight in God's Word, and will continue to believe it fully. Those who do not believe and delight in God's Word give evidence that they are not "of God."

Another evidence of genuine salvation is a continuing present relationship with Jesus Christ. Jesus says, "Abide in me, and I in you" and, "If you abide in me, and my words abide in you, ask whatever you will, and it shall be done for you" (John 15:4, 7). This abiding in Christ will include not only day-by-day trust in him in various situations, but also certainly regular fellowship with him in prayer and worship.

Finally, a major area of evidence that we are genuine believers is found in a life of obedience to God's commands. John says, "He who says 'I know him' but disobeys his commandments is a liar, and the truth is not in him; but whoever keeps his word, in him truly love for God is perfected. By this we may be sure that we are in him: he who says he abides in him ought to walk in the same way in which he walked" (1 John 2:4-6). A perfect life is not necessary, of course. John is rather saying that in general our lives ought to be ones of imitation of Christ and likeness to him in what we do and say. If we have genuine saving faith, there will be clear results in obedience in our lives (see also 1 John 3:9-10, 24; 1 John 5:18). Thus James can say, "Faith by itself, if it has no works, is dead" and "I by my works will show you my faith" (James 2:17-18). One large area of obedience to God includes love for fellow Christians. "He who loves his brother abides in the light" (1 John 2:10). "We know that we have passed out of death into life, because we love the brethren. He who does not love abides in death" (1 John 3:14, cf. 1 John 3:17; 1 John 4:7). One evidence of this love is continuing in

> **"Jesus says, 'Abide in me, and I in you'... This abiding in Christ will include not only day-by-day trust in him in various situations, but also certainly regular fellowship with him in prayer and worship."**
>
> —WAYNE GRUDEM

Christian fellowship (1 John 2:19), and another is giving to a brother in need (1 John 3:17; cf. Matthew 25:31-46).

3. Do I See a Long-Term Pattern of Growth in My Christian Life?

The first two areas of assurance dealt with present faith and present evidence of the Holy Spirit at work in our lives. But Peter gives one more kind of test that we can use to ask whether we are genuinely believers. He tells us that there are some character traits which, if we keep on increasing in them, will guarantee that we will "never fall" (2 Peter 1:10). He tells his readers to add to their faith virtue, knowledge, self-control, steadfastness, godliness, brotherly affection, love (2 Peter 1:5-7). Then he says that these things are to belong to his readers and to continually "abound" in their lives (2 Peter 1:8). He adds that they are to "be the more zealous to confirm your call and election" and says then that *"if you do this* (literally, "these things," referring to the character traits mentioned in vv. 5-7) *you will never fall"* (2 Peter 1:10).

The way that we confirm our call and election, then, is to continue to grow in "these things." This implies that our assurance of salvation can be something that increases over time in our lives. Every year that we add to these character traits in our lives, we gain greater and greater assurance of our salvation. Thus, though young believers can have a quite strong confidence in their salvation, that assurance can increase to even deeper certainty over the years in which they grow toward Christian maturity.[20] If they continue to add these things they will confirm their call and election and will "never fall."

The result of these three questions that we can ask ourselves should be to give strong assurance to those who are genuinely believers. In this way the doctrine of the perseverance of the saints will be a tremendously

---

[20] Cf. 1 Tim. 3:13, which says, that those who have "served well" as deacons gain "greater assurance in their faith in Christ Jesus" (NIV)

comforting doctrine. No one who has such assurance should wonder, "Will I be able to persevere to the end of my life and therefore be saved?" Everyone who gains assurance through such a self-examination should rather think, "I am truly born again; therefore, I will certainly persevere to the end, because I am being guarded 'by God's power' working through my faith (1 Peter 1:5) and therefore I will never be lost. Jesus will raise me up at the last day and I will enter into his kingdom forever" (John 6:40).

On the other hand, this doctrine of the perseverance of the saints, if rightly understood, should cause genuine worry, and even fear, in the hearts of any who are "backsliding" or straying away from Christ. Such persons must clearly be warned that only those who persevere to the end have been truly born again. If they fall away from their profession of faith in Christ and life of obedience to him, they may not really be saved—in fact, the *evidence* that they are giving *is that they are not saved* and they never really were saved. Once they stop trusting in Christ and obeying him (I am speaking in terms of outward evidence) they have no genuine assurance of salvation, and

> **"Everyone who gains assurance through such a self-examination should rather think, 'I am truly born again; therefore, I will certainly persevere to the end, because I am being guarded "by God's power" working through my faith (1 Peter 1:5) and therefore I will never be lost. Jesus will raise me up at the last day and I will enter into his kingdom forever' (John 6:40)."**
>
> —WAYNE GRUDEM

they should consider themselves unsaved, and turn to Christ in repentance and ask him for forgiveness of their sins.

At this point, in terms of pastoral care with those who have strayed away from their Christian profession, we should realize that *Calvinists* and *Arminians* (those who believe in the perseverance of the saints and those who think that Christians can lose their salvation) *will both counsel a "backslider" in the same way*. According to the Arminian this person was a Christian at one time but is no longer a Christian. According to the Calvinist, such a person never really was a Christian in the first place and is not one now. But in both cases the biblical counsel given would be the same: "You do not appear to be a Christian now—you must repent of your sins and trust in Christ for your salvation!" Though the Calvinist and Arminian would differ on their interpretation of the previous history, they would agree on what should be done in the present.[21]

But here we see why the phrase *eternal security* can be quite misleading. In some evangelical churches, instead of teaching the full and balanced presentation of the doctrine of the perseverance of the saints, pastors have sometimes taught a watered-down version, which in effect tells people that all who have once made a profession of faith and been baptized are "eternally secure." The result is that some people who are not genuinely converted at all may "come forward" at the end of an evangelistic sermon to profess faith in Christ, and may be baptized shortly after that, but then they leave the fellowship of the church and live a life no different from the one they lived before they gained this "eternal security." In this way people are given false assurance and are being cruelly deceived into thinking they are going to heaven when in fact they are not.[22]

---

[21] Of course, both the Calvinist and the Arminian would allow for the possibility that the "backslidden" person is truly born again and has just fallen into sin and doubt. But both would agree that it is pastorally wise to assume that the person is not a Christian until some evidence of present faith is forthcoming.

[22] Of course, not all who use the phrase eternal security make mistakes of this sort, but the phrase is certainly open to such misunderstanding.

Recommended Resources

Big, Bold, Biblical Prayers for the Next Generation

The needs of the next generation, the challenges they face, and the opportunities before them are great. What might God be pleased to do if His people come to Him with BIG, BOLD, BIBLICAL prayers of faith? *Big, Bold, Biblical Prayers for the Next Generation* challenges parents, grandparents, pastors, children's ministry leaders, teachers, and all who care about the next generation to intentionally pray for the children in their family, church, and around the world. David Michael casts a vision for how and why we need to pray big, bold, biblical prayers, and provides 17 prayers you can join him in praying for the next generation along with relevant Scripture passages to spark your prayers.

A Father's Guide to Blessing His Children

A blessing is a biblical way to express hope and vision for what a child will become. In one sense, it is a prayer asking God to make that hope and vision true for a child. It is also an opportunity to look a child in the eye and express your hope and vision for his or her life. The 29 blessings in this booklet provide a model for creating blessings of your own. Since each blessing is rooted in Scripture, this is another way to pray biblical prayers for your children and give them a biblical vision for their lives. As David Michael reflects on his experience as a pastor, father, and grandfather, he has witnessed more fruit from blessing others in this way than almost anything else he has done.

Helping Children to Understand the Gospel

The gospel is the most important truth one generation can communicate to the next, and God calls parents and teachers to be wise sowers. This calls for accurate, discerning, and intentional practices of cultivating, teaching, and praying in the hope that God, who gives the growth, will work in children's hearts to yield hundredfold harvests of faith. This booklet includes a 10-week family devotional, "Ten Essential Gospel Truths," to help parents explain the gospel to their children. Other topics explored include: preparing the hearts of children to hear the gospel, discerning stages of spiritual growth, communicating the essential truths of the gospel message, and presenting the gospel in an accurate and child-friendly manner.

Glorious God, Glorious Gospel
An Interactive Family Devotional

Glorious God, Glorious Gospel is an interactive family devotional designed to help parents ground their children in the essential, foundational, and glorious truths of the gospel. These truths take into account the whole counsel of God and answer important questions, such as: *Who is God, and what is He like? Why do I exist? How am I to act toward God? What is my greatest problem and need? How can I be saved? How should I now live?* The interactive format is meant to encourage your children toward life-transforming faith in Christ by guiding, inspiring, and imploring them to personally and sincerely respond to God's truth with their minds, hearts, and wills. A coloring book and notebook are available as companion pieces to further engage young children and elementary-age children.

About Truth78

Truth78 is a vision-oriented ministry for the next generations. Our vision is that the next generations know, honor, and treasure God, setting their hope in Christ alone, so that they will live as faithful disciples for the glory of God.

Our mission is to nurture the faith of the next generations by equipping the church and home with resources and training that instruct the mind, engage the heart, and influence the will through proclaiming the whole counsel of God.

Our resources and training are developed to be God-centered, Bible-saturated, gospel-focused, Christ-exalting, Spirit-dependent, doctrinally grounded, and discipleship-oriented.

Resources for Church and Home

Truth78 offers the following categories of resources and training materials for equipping the church and home:

Vision-Casting and Training—We offer a wide variety of booklets, video and audio seminars, articles, and other practical training resources that highlight and further expound our vision, mission, and values, as well as our educational philosophy and methodology. Many of these resources are freely distributed through our website to help ministry leaders, volunteers, and parents implement Truth78's vision and mission in their churches and homes.

Curriculum—We publish materials designed for formal Bible instruction. The scope and sequence of these materials reflects our commitment to teach children and youth the whole counsel of God over the course of their education. Materials include curricula for Sunday schools, Midweek Bible programs, Backyard Bible Clubs or Vacation Bible Schools, and Intergenerational studies. Most of these materials can be adapted for use in Christian schools and education in the home.

Parenting and Family Discipleship—We have produced a variety of materials and training resources designed to help parents disciple their children, including booklets, video presentations, family devotionals, children's books, articles, and other recommended resources. Our curricula also include parent pages to help parents apply what is taught in the classroom to their child's daily experience in order to nurture faith.

Bible Memory—Our Fighter Verses Bible memory program is designed to encourage churches, families, and individuals in the lifelong practice and love of Bible memory. The program offers an easy-to-use Bible memory system with carefully chosen verses to help fight the fight of faith. It is available in print, on FighterVerses.com, and as an app for smartphones and other mobile devices. For pre-readers, Foundation Verses uses simple images to help young children memorize 76 key verses. We also offer a study that corresponds to Set 1 of the Fighter Verses. Visit FighterVerses.com for more on the Fighter Verses Study, as well as a weekly devotional blog and free memory aids.

Nonprofit Ministry

Truth78 is a 501(c)(3) nonprofit ministry structured to tell "the glorious deeds of the LORD, and his might, and the wonders that he has done" (Psalm 78:4) to millions of children and youth in the next generation who do not know, honor, and treasure Jesus Christ. Ministry supporters make it possible to reach more children of the next generation globally through...

- Funding curriculum translation projects and offering translated resources for free distribution through our website.

- Providing free training materials to equip children's and youth ministry leaders, volunteers, and parents to develop a biblical vision for their ministry to the next generation, and to provide specific training on using our resources and on the roles and functions of children's and youth ministry.

- Underwriting a fund to help ministries and individuals unable to fully afford Truth78 resources.

For more information on Truth78 or any of these initiatives, visit Truth78.org.